Fall Changes

by Kaye Gager

Scott Foresman
is an imprint of

Glenview, Illinois • Boston, Massachusetts • Mesa, Arizona
Shoreview, Minnesota • Upper Saddle River, New Jersey

Photographs
Every effort has been made to secure permission and provide appropriate credit for photographic material. The publisher deeply regrets any omission and pledges to correct errors called to its attention in subsequent editions.

Unless otherwise acknowledged, all photographs are the property of Pearson Education, Inc.

Photo locators denoted as follows: Top (T), Center (C), Bottom (B), Left (L), Right (R), Background (Bkgd).

Cover: ©Gary W. Carter/Corbis; **Title Page:** ©David W. Hamilton/Getty Images; 3 ©Chase Swift/Corbis; 4 ©Markus Varesvuo/Nature Picture Library; 5 ©David W. Hamilton/Getty Images; 6 ©Michael Durham/Getty Images; 7 ©Gary W. Carter/Corbis; 8 (TL) Getty Images,(TR) ©Thorsten Milse/Getty Images,(BR) ©Tom Bean/Getty Images,(BL) ©Peter Lilja/Getty Images

ISBN 13: 978-0-328-39320-6
ISBN 10:   0-328-39320-7

In the fall, some birds fly
to warmer places.
They leave before it gets colder.

Some animals stay.
This bird does not fly away.
It stays right here all winter.

Some animals grow new fur.
This fox is ready for the
coldest day.
He won't be cold.

Some animals build new
homes.
This beaver builds a home.
It is on the edge of a river.

In the fall, animals need food.
The food must last until spring.
This chipmunk finds nuts.

Now we say good-bye to fall.

The air is getting colder.

Are the animals ready for winter?

Oh, yes, they are ready!